My Mother's Keeper

My Mother's Keeper

Jean Williams

More poems by Jean Williams: *The Abundance of Simplicity*, 2013.

Copyright © 2021 by the author.
All rights reserved. No part of this book may be used or reproduced in any manner whatsoever without written permission, except in the case of brief quotations embedded in critical articles or reviews.

Published in 2021
Printed in the United States

ISBN 978-1-7374215-1-1

For my sisters

Contents

The Tallest Tree 1
My Year of Silence 2
Assisted Living 3
Cat 4
People of Good Character 5
There Is No Instruction Manual for Ghosts 6
How to Love When It's Difficult 7
A Present to Herself 9
Poem for Abandoned Children 10
Long-Range Perspective 12
Poems Are Like Obon Lanterns 13
Making Love 14
Avoiding Traps 16
To a Child Half-Grown 17
Elderly Mother 18
It Is Not Easy to Die 20
People Who Have Been Hurt 21
Ambivalence at Mother's Deathbed 22
December Child 24

Memories of Being a Parent	26
My Birth	28
Sweet Revenge	30
Nursing the Baby	31
Dream of a Black Lacquer Bed	32
Open Season	35
Requiem	37
Dark Matters	39
Doing Time	40
Wild Baby Rabbits	42
Russian Woman	43
The Perfect Victim	44
Playing Baby	45
A Peaceful Devon Home	46
Before the Birth	47
A Small Child's View of the World	48
Vertigo	51
View from the Ledge	53
Long Days at the Farm	55
A Brittle Personality	57
Inch by Inch	58
No Visible Bruises	59
Near the End of Life	60
In the Concentration Camp	61
Too Tired	63

Collateral Damage 64
A Woman Disguised as a Normal Person 65
Writing Poems 67
Legacy 68

The Tallest Tree

The enormous redwood
in our backyard
gave its all to the soil around it,
to bushes and flowers
even though, underground, its roots
had rotted clear through
and its branches were stiff and dry.

The night of the big storm,
its roots could not hold it upright any longer.
Like my father in his declining years,
the tree let go of the earth gradually
and rolled off the roof with a sigh,
splintering branch after branch
and easing down onto the ground so softly
that no one in the house was frightened.

My Year of Silence

Whatever I say
gets me into trouble.
So I say nothing.

Have you learned your lesson?
they ask.
Why are you so strange?
they ask.

Words smolder inside me,
but I have the pride of broken things.
I say nothing.

But I am still in here.
I am alive.

My face is a mirror
that takes in emotions
and suffocates them.

Assisted Living

At ninety-seven, Mother lives
in a velvet-lined box,
like her heart-shaped locket
with Dad's picture inside.
The carpeted hallways are lonely.
In the darkening forest of her mind,
most of life is out of reach.
All she has to do now is be herself.
She drinks her day in sips.

Cat

Mother was like a cat that climbed
up a bookcase or the refrigerator
to perch higher than anyone else.
Grandmas and disapproving aunts
waited outside the house like ambulances
while Mother leapt from counter to stove,
saying that we children were hers
and she wanted no outside interference.

Daddy was a calming presence
but she hissed and spat at him,
demanding to know
how she could be expected
to land on her feet as a good mother
with so many hostile eyes
watching through the window.

People of Good Character

How can I teach my children
a lesson they will never forget?
I read in some article
that it takes six minutes without oxygen
before a child is really dead,
so probably two minutes
of not being able to breathe
would not be too dangerous.
I'll be able to tell by their eyes
if they're about to pass out.

Someday I hope they understand
all the things I was forced to do
to correct their bad behavior
and help them grow up to be
people of good character.

There Is No Instruction Manual for Ghosts

My old house calls me back,
but the people I love
do not recognize me.
I smell dinner cooking
and am not hungry.
I see comfortable beds
but do not want to sleep.

Everything seems strange.
I have no pockets.
I have no teeth, only eyes.
I circle the living room
and float out through the door.

How to Love When It's Difficult

From somewhere deep inside me
I hear footsteps.
It's Mother.
She wants me to forgive her.
I never intended to be mean, she says.
I was just an ordinary person longing for love.

I shift from foot to foot.
Her voice has the right tones, the right words,
but she is not sorry for anything,
cannot comprehend why I might hold a grudge.
Surely it is time to unclench my heart,
to stop prowling around like a refugee
foraging for bread.

But if I allow myself to feel
the love we have for each other,
I will also remember the hatred,
the mutual contempt, the ominous silences,
the lack of understanding between us.

cont.

It is an eternal question: how to pivot,
how to reclaim what is valuable from long ago
without flaunting the wounds.

What I need is a way to distill the past,
to pour my memories through a filter
and heat them in a retort
until they are concentrated and purified,
until pain is drawn off and
only the meaningful part is left.

A Present to Herself

Mother was mean to us children
as a present to herself.

When you need to protect yourself
from someone you love, it hardens you.

My sisters and I are grown now
and we almost feel safe.

But how can she ever forgive us,
we who remember those dark times?

Poem for Abandoned Children

In hours of despair and loneliness,
close your eyes. Imagine
that some kind, enormous being
is cradling you
as if you were precious.

No matter how many years it has been
since your parents passed away
or became estranged,
your body will remember
the feeling of adult arms around you.

When you were a baby
they cared for you gently.
They delighted in each tiny expression,
each sigh and grunt and coo.
Their warmth surrounded you
like a fragrance
and dissolved into your cells.

cont.

No matter what has happened,
some inner part of them still feels love
and reaches out to embrace you.

Long-Range Perspective

The houses that knew me are gone —
pulled apart for lumber,
bulldozed into abandoned cellars.

The frosted window panes,
buckets under leaky ceilings,
the closet
that smelled of Daddy's Sunday hat,
the threadbare, dark red linoleum,
the treadle sewing machine,
the tick-tick of our spaniel's feet
racing to the door,
the thicket of lilac bushes …

My childhood homes
have turned into stories,
glowing from within
like clouds in front of the sun.

Poems Are Like Obon Lanterns

People write poems
so they can remember things
or so they can forget,
whichever they need to do.

Look, someone has written another poem
and is sending it out across the water.

(In traditional Japan, at the end of the Obon season, families thank their ancestors for visiting and protecting them by sending floating lanterns down the river or out to sea.)

Making Love

touching you, I feel quiet inside
we study each other
discover our fingers
there is nothing else we want to know
you relax under my hands
I am inventing you
you are inventing me

we forget about the leak in the tire
ingrown toenails
to-do lists
being overweight
all we know is surrender
you can't be mad at someone
whose belly you are stroking

cont.

we forget we must get up tomorrow
who needs sleep
your laugh deepens
like in a movie scene
we touch the petals of joy
hold our feelings up to the light
we have forgotten how to be hungry

making love is the best meditation
it focuses the mind
we experience each other moment by moment
no regrets, no predictions
just being together
is enough
you run your finger along my arm

Avoiding Traps

Mother, you wanted to put us in a box,
instant love whenever you wanted it.
Even as toddlers, we found ways
to slip through the cracks.
We scampered through the weeds
and let our feelings come and go
without examination. When older,
going to school was a refuge.

It must have been hard for you
to struggle for happiness
in the midst of poverty.
We know there were years
when you folded away wedding gifts
too beautiful to use.

In old age, you implore us to come closer.
The house is too big now, too quiet.
Your fretful hands reach out for an embrace.
Your withered face is radiant with welcome.
We sit politely on your living room couch
but inside us, the story is the same as before —
we dart away and refuse to be tempted.

To a Child Half-Grown

My precious daughter,
don't try to scrub my smell
from your skin.

Girl, this line of women
goes back a long way.
We are teachers and midwives.
We love all our children
— even those who bite and scratch.

We are gardeners of time.
We ignore drought
and wait for harvest.

When you reject me so furiously,
I suffer the vanities of motherhood,
but I can see you are a warrior.

Elderly Mother

As she grows closer to the earth,
she is never hungry but always tired.
Her thin arms are bruised
from bumping into the furniture.
Her body has shrunk to its core
as she grimly holds onto what she's got.

At Mother's house we see
untended flower beds,
misplaced letters and photos,
discarded, mud-splattered shoes.
She staggers through each chilly night
with cramps in her hands and feet,
gets up, looks at the clock,
tries again to sleep.

My sisters and I try to help her
but she denies she needs help.
She leans too close to the flame
when she checks the ham and beans,
and we hesitate to interfere.

cont.

Paperwork piles up in the clothes closet.
She cannot balance her checkbook
or reset the blinking alarm clock.
She answers the phone, feeds the cat,
and replies to junk mail.
She rages against jars that won't open,
video buttons that don't click on.
She decides that from now on,
she will wear only her favorite clothes.

Another bad fall.
A pan of soup splashes onto the floor,
and wiping it up makes her heart pound painfully.
She rejects the walker, the senior-center bus.
She forgets what happened
but remembers how she felt.

We daughters talk with one another.
We try not to provoke her.
What to do. What to do.
We wait. We worry.

It Is Not Easy to Die

As I close my eyes
and push the scaffolding of life away,
what remains most clearly in my mind
are people. It comforts me
to think of those, alive and dead,
whom I knew best.
They slide silently into their places,
a tableau in amber.

My skin is smooth as tulips,
my lips are dry,
my eyelashes crusted.
My limbs grow numb,
my heart whirs laboriously in my chest,
the blood thick and slow.
Yet to everyone else in the world,
this is just an ordinary day,
a day like any other.

People Who Have Been Hurt

The people Mother loved best
were those who had been hurt.
She bent toward them lovingly.
She comforted them.

If we children were loud or disobedient,
if we swaggered around or acted smug,
she was enraged,
felt we needed to be taken down a peg.
We had to be punished.

Then after she had made us cry
she would talk to us kindly.
She saw that as her noblest role in life,
consoling people who had been hurt.

Ambivalence at Mother's Deathbed

Mother, we kneel beside your bed
as if tending a grave.
We moisten your lips
and stroke your hands.

You would have loved all this attention,
the hushed deference,
the respect for your needs.
Rest now.
No need any longer for you to struggle
with the details of living.

You may not even be aware
that we are in this room
but it does not matter.
We love you —
the person who gave us life.

cont.

Evening turns into night
as we sit beside your bed.
Your body looks exhausted, depleted.
Our memories page through the years.
Our hands smooth your hair
and gently wipe sweat from your brow.

We were not only your daughters,
we were your emotional food,
but the threats that frightened us as children
are hollow tonight,
and you too probably feel a sense of relief
— our journey together is nearing an end.

December Child

I was born in December,
the month of cold rain,
of buckets set out in the living room
to catch drips from the ceiling,
a month of scarves and sweaters
and flannel-lined jeans
and wind that made the windows rattle.
Mother pressed rags under the front door
and into window sills.
We slept under thick wool comforters.
Out on the porch, at the washing machine,
Mother fed diapers through the wringer.

Winter is the season
when weaklings die quickly, discreetly,
not calling undue attention to themselves.
Snow covers trash heaps and bare gardens.
Colors dissolve into shades of gray
and on clear nights the stars seem very near.
The wind blows soot and dust
in featherlike patterns across the snowdrifts.

cont.

I have always liked winter,
being dressed in hat and mittens
and feeling a cold breeze on my face.
Like a Viking child, I always loved snow,
liked the feeling of toughing it out,
of being strong, being prepared,
being a pioneer, an Alaskan trapper,
or a hunter striding through the woods
a long way from camp.

Memories of Being a Parent

Ah, the baby years
— the heat of small bodies,
the intensity of tasting and touching,
baby rubble strewn through the living room,
someone clinging to my leg
as I stood cooking at the stove.

I remember the later years too
— jeans with holes in the knees,
camp-outs, dams in the creek,
holding the fearless wild bird
in my cupped hands,
the baby mouse, basket weaving,
a sewing machine run at reckless speed,
decorating the plastic Christmas tree in August
the year she had chicken pox.

cont.

Then there were the hilarious sowbugs,
Asterix and Obelix,
who enjoyed jumping from rock to rock
and the other sowbug, Josephine,
who ran madly across the table,
stopped abruptly, then peered over the edge
and hurried in the opposite direction.
And let me tell you about the slippery-slide
we made for the snails …

(Sowbugs are also known as pillbugs.)

My Birth

As an hours-old newborn,
I was carried into Mother's hospital room.
The nurse laid me down and fled,
uncertain what to say.
Mother said to herself,
"Well, this is my new baby.
Let me unwrap her blanket
and take a look."

Unfolding the blanket,
Mother was stunned to see
the baby's misshapen hips and twisted foot.
"Oh God," she thought,
"I tried to do everything right
and here I've given birth to a freak!"
She screamed and screamed
until a nurse ran in
and carried me away.

cont.

I was a teenager
when Mother told me this story.
Seeing the shock on my face,
she laughed and laughed.

Is a flawed child harder to love,
like a porcelain doll with a cracked face?

Then she said, "Just kidding!
Of course, when I first saw you
and noticed those poor little legs,
my heart overflowed with love.
I picked you up and held you close."

Sweet Revenge

When Mother felt we children
did not respect her enough,
were getting too independent,
she led us away from fresh water
and into the swamp.

"Follow me," she cried gaily,
striding toward the brackish water.
"Trust me — step where I step
and we'll have a picnic on the other side.
Under the surface of the water
there are tree stumps spread about
and I know where they are.
But be very careful where you put your feet
Otherwise you might fall in and drown."

Cold water came up to our ankles
and the air had the rancid tang of decay.
We had no choice but to follow.
Mother was thrilled.
She had outwitted us.

Nursing the Baby

My little nestling
tugs at wisps of her hair,
burrows into my breast.
Drawing out milk,
panting for air,
over and over, in rhythm.
I never knew
that nursing could be so athletic.
Steamy heat
radiates from her body.
Her feet tap against my arm.
Gulp, pant, gulp, pant.
She is completely absorbed
in the task of eating.

Dream of a Black Lacquer Bed
(after Du Fu)

Many nights the household was roused from sleep
by the whinny of horses. Servants came with lanterns.
I dressed quickly; my young wife wept. Parting
the silk gauze bed-hangings, I kissed her and strode
into the courtyard. My boots rang on the cobblestones.
Servants handed me a riding crop and opened the gate
for courtiers bringing orders from the emperor.

Years went by. Often, as I crossed dark rivers
or stumbled along mountain paths, I sighed
for the serenity of old age, when I would be able
to sit at ease with my wife and a cup of wine.
Wearing soft shoes, we would watch passing clouds,
no one calling my name. I would be undisturbed
by thoughts of wind and rain, and listen only
to the faraway sound of wild geese flying south.

cont.

But now it is too late. My eyes have grown dim,
and there is a painful pressure in my chest.
Doctors mix herbal tinctures and shake their heads.
Friends whisper at the door. Servants come and go.
I know that I am dying. Perhaps at last I can have
the one thing in the world I long for: to see
my wife's breasts in the daylight — just she and I
alone, no doctors or servants or relatives.

My wife's eyes widen with surprise. She says
it is impossible because of the servants… besides,
she is ashamed of her body, no longer young.
But as master of this house, I give the order:
only from my wife's hands will I take a sip
of wine or medicine. No one else may be in the room.
The servants protest. It is against custom,
and what if they are needed for something urgent?

cont.

The big wooden door is closed. We laugh quietly,
she and I. Until now, we have never been alone.
Even at night, two servants slept in our room.
Now, the servants wait just outside the door
but they cannot hear us, cannot see us. My wife
pushes the embroidered bed-hangings aside
and opens the shutters. From my bed I can see
the dark wooden walls, bare and dusty.

In silent sadness, my wife touches my hand.
Then she places her headdress on the cabinet
and loosens her clothing, letting the silk
tunic and under-tunic fall from her shoulders.
I am overwhelmed by her beauty and her love.
No need for talk, just peacefully being together.
As I leave this world, I am comforted by the silky feel
of my wife's hair, the softness of her breasts.

Open Season

It was to be open season on parents
once we were adults,
our confidence back on a firm footing.
We thought that one day
we could meet them as equals
and ask hard questions,
telling them frankly how things had been for us.
The whole trash pile of resentments
that had been pushed to one side
would eventually be unearthed,
acknowledged, and dealt with.

But we miscalculated.
Our parents at eighty seem fragile and sweet,
and if we bring up the past,
what they remember most is how they suffered,
how hard they tried,
and the great love they felt for us.
We hesitate,
feeling protective of their health and sanity.

cont.

They would never be able to explain
why they acted as they did,
and guesses or excuses would give us no satisfaction.
The ghost ship of restitution will never arrive.
Love and heartache have become all mixed together.

Requiem

Through a small window, Mother,
I can look back to my earliest years,
before our family was irretrievably changed
by your instability,
before you hated the unfeminine way I laughed,
before A's on my report card
became war trophies spread out for your approval.
We children walked barefoot along a dirt path,
avoiding unexpected blows and sand burrs.

Just forget all this, you said.
Wash out those memories with soap
and hang them, like cups, back in the cupboard.
What you saw with your own eyes
never happened.

cont.

It was a life without guardrails,
a dance marathon that exhausted us all.
You wanted us to stop being sassy,
to be too scared of you to disobey.
You wanted Dad to come running,
to beg you to calm down,
and to prove once and for all
that he loved you
more than he loved us children.

Dark Matters

I carry my mother inside my body
like an underdeveloped fetus,
a heaviness that I cannot cast out.
Although I practice deep breathing
and cling to bravado,
her words hole up in a corner of my mind,
ready to be reassembled.
They stiffen and twitch
at any small movement of air.

I tell myself I can brazen out such memories,
but during any lull in hostilities
my darkness quivers like piano wire.

Doing Time

Each of us sisters reacted differently
to the stressful situation at home —
one girl's hair fell out from stress,
another referred to herself
in the third person,
and I did not speak for a year.

Mother loved us very much
but what I remember most
is how we three girls stood rigid
in the searchlight of Mother's attention.
If we flinched or ducked, it made her angry.
In that isolated farmhouse
her anger ricocheted off the walls.

You act like I'm a monster,
but really I'm a good person.
And don't ever tell your father about this
because if you do,
I'll make sure that it hurts him much more
than you could ever hurt me.

cont.

I am a good daughter.
I will not cut anyone's face out of photographs.
Perhaps I should tell these stories in a cheerier way.

Wild Baby Rabbits

Being in the house with Mother,
who was charming and pretty and patient
and who loved us very much
yet in many ways was a failure as a mother —

It felt like the time my sisters and I
squatted around a cardboard box
holding the nest of baby rabbits
that Daddy brought in from the field,
a ring of our bare toes
surrounding the box of rags.
How wonderful those rabbits were —
perfect little baby faces and paws and tails.
We stroked them and loved them.
It was a special, enchanted time.
Their eyes were alert and shining.
The bunnies sniffed at our fingers
and slept together in a pile.
We were going to keep them as pets
but we didn't have the right kind of milk.

If only we could have saved them.

Russian Woman

"I have always been afraid,"
Lana whispered
as her mind began to slip.
She continued long walks in all weather,
this vigorous, intelligent woman
who had traveled half the world
to forge a new life in San Francisco
and now could hardly find her way home.
It took her hours to make cabbage soup.
When household bills arrived,
she stacked them neatly on the kitchen counter.
She gave piano lessons as usual
and phoned friends only on her 'good' days.

But at night she lay awake, eyes open.
She knew.

The Perfect Victim
for Mother

The last child in the family,
her birth almost killed her mother.
As a girl, she sat on the porch swing
with a stack of limp paperbacks,
staying out of everyone's way and being quiet.
In winter, she stood at the frosted window
as snow fell in clumps from dark branches,
her small face pressed against the glass.

She dreamed of a time when she
would be beautiful and charming and loved,
when she would have to wash fewer dishes,
when she wouldn't have to sleep with a sister
who wet the bed. Luckily, an uncle
took pity on her and told her she was special.

Playing Baby

After a day full of petty squabbles
my sister and I would go upstairs to bed.
Away from our parents, we spat out
angry words about how much we hated each other
and, for the ultimate insult,
we pointed our bare fannies at each other.

You girls pipe down up there and go to sleep.

After we tired of talking,
the two of us played baby,
suckling each other's flat breasts.
When pretending to be the mother,
it was kind of fun to cuddle the little one in,
although it did feel ticklish and weird
to have your nipples sucked.
What each of us liked best
was to be the baby.

A Peaceful Devon Home

The neighbors' kitchen
had the spare look of a house
where no one reads —
a 1940s clock on the wall,
a yellow refrigerator with rounded corners,
an advertising calendar hung from a nail.
Their son and his wife, who were visiting,
rose eagerly to offer us a seat
(they had only four chairs).
We said no, no, don't get up.
We just stopped by for a moment.

The eighteen-month-old grandson
was sleeping on a blanket
in the middle of the kitchen table,
an adult on each side
so the child wouldn't roll off.
The four adults talked quietly
and watched the baby with adoring eyes,
waiting for him to wake up.

Before the Birth

Someone I have never met
touches me from inside my body
— delicately, calmly, with tiny hands.

Our blood and breath commingle.
My baby watches shadows in dim light
and listens to aquarium voices.
He hunches down and stretches out.
Blood spurts from one chamber of his heart
to another, gathering strength.
Soon he will emerge into the air and unfurl.

A Small Child's View of the World

Where's Mama's shoe?
Here it is!
Mama shoe, baby shoe.
Mama coat, baby coat.
All gone.
All gone.

When Mama holds me against her,
her voice buzzes in my chest.
Good things occur, and bad things,
but I never worry, because soon —
something else will happen.
Sensations and impulses and experiences
flow through me like water
and swirl past.

I wake up happy every day
and run to see what is going on.
I hold out my arms and legs
to be dressed and undressed.

cont.

Awakening in the night,
I find myself upside-down
over a steaming tea kettle
to soothe my cough.
I love being read to, having things explained,
paging through the Montgomery Ward catalog.
Look — everything has a name!

Part of the floor is warm, another part cool.
Some ladies have chewing gum in their purses.
I clamber over people's feet
and sit on a box to eat at the table.
I spill my milk, drop spoons.
I grasp the edge of the bed at night
to keep from falling out of bed.
Life is a blur of grandmas and food,
having my face washed, my nose blown.

Whazzat?
Lemme see!

I run toward life,
noticing everything around me
without analyzing it.

cont.

Over the years though
my reactions have become saturated
with grown-up thoughts.
What did they mean by that?
Think before you act.
Look what you have done.

The glistening world of early childhood.
All gone.
All gone.

Vertigo

This is how it starts:
Mother calls us her sweethearts.
She says she would never do anything
to hurt us.
But she cannot help saying
what she really thinks about our behavior.
Her nostrils flare.
An odd flicker comes into her eyes.
She shakes our shoulders,
pushes us onto chairs.

We sit very, very still,
our faces blank, our eyes dull.
When you are really afraid
it feels like your hair is starting to burn.

I can't remember the next part.

cont.

Darkness has settled around the farm.
It is time to reheat the soup
and cut slices of bread from the loaf.
Mother is still explaining
why we are very bad children,
but usually Dad comes in for supper
before things go too far.

View from the Ledge

*The small bones of children
heal quickly, they say.
And children do not remember
anything that happens to them
when they are very young.*

What are you supposed to think
if your mother tries to kill you?
(Just once or twice, though.)

The decade of her blue floral housecoat
was even grimmer than the decade
of her quilted red housecoat.
Mother's moods shifted abruptly;
she might lash out at remarks or deeds
she would have laughed off
a few minutes or hours before.

cont.

At last I am old enough to leave.
I'm afraid though
that it may take me some time to calm down.
I touch the wall to steady myself.
I had not expected to be alive.
I had not expected to be myself.

I had two mothers —
the nice one whom I loved
and the bad one,
whom I also loved.

I didn't tell the nice one
about the bad one
because it would have made her sad.
And I didn't tell the bad one about the other
because it would have made her angry.

When the nice mother was there
I held onto her leg,
trying to make her stay,
and when the bad one came,
I climbed into a cardboard box
and pulled the lid shut.

Long Days at the Farm

The baby was asleep in the bedroom
and I watched from a chair
as Mother washed the floorboards
on her knees, singing a hymn.

As best she could,
she filled the space
where a mother should be.
But sometimes she stood silently
at the window, waiting for Dad
to come home on the tractor.

cont.

She never left us alone
or hungry.
We wore clean clothes
and had new shoes for Easter.
She baked four loaves of bread
each Saturday
and polished the furniture.
She hung out the wash
on the weed-stubble lawn
as a cold wind blew.

I watched how she struggled
and knew she was doing her best.
I did not hate her
in those early years.

A Brittle Personality

act normal, Mother says
she wants   she wants
to love herself
in the mirror of my eyes
for us to be
one spirit   in two voices

as my own breasts begin to grow
her soft, feminine body
which was once   my home
seems very foreign
she reaches out   presses against me
with gummy fingers
her hugs   are too tight

Inch by Inch

Over the long haul
I would not recommend
embarrassment
as a way of life
but if you grow up
in the Midwest
you learn to absorb
other people's outbursts
with silence.
You hold your own thoughts
deep inside like a snail,
transforming bits of reality
into a shell.

No Visible Bruises

Someone who loves us
is also our enemy.
We children twist and turn,
counting the blows.
We smooth our expressions
because we like to believe
that we live in a functioning family.

An internal light flashes every six seconds
telling us that there is no reason to fear
and that no one is getting hurt, not *really*.

Near the End of Life

I tried to be a good mother.
I wanted to be the one
who knew what to do.
I wanted to be a mother my children loved.

Despite my good intentions
things went out of control.
I had to protect myself from them.
Being a mother
was not supposed to be this hard.

Each evening when I turned out the light
I lay in bed drowning in a silent river
of sorry   sorry   sorry

But at least I was true to my real feelings —
and no one was ever able to stop me.

In the Concentration Camp

After a rain
the children formed toys
from the clay-like mud:
little horses and rabbits and cats.
Never dogs —
too scary.
When the mud animals dried
the children played with them.

The other thing
they made from mud
was pretend food:
round balls for apples,
flat pieces for bread,
oblong bananas,
triangular pieces of cake,
pebble-sized grapes.

cont.

The children kept their mud toys
in a small cardboard box
and when waiting in the cold
for their evening meal,
they lined up the mud animals
and told them:
come, eat.

Too Tired

when I walk slowly and with effort
I forgive my legs
when my fingers are stiff from working
I am kind to my fingers
when I come to the end of what I can do
I say thank you to my body
just carry on without me
write soon

Collateral Damage

Even if I do bad things sometimes,
it hurts me to do them.
That must mean I am not really evil.

When Mother threw a fit,
we kids scattered like roaches.
We stopped trying
to make some sense of it all
and wrapped ourselves in sarcasm,
shrieking with laughter,
afraid of nobody.

Eventually we sobered up
and realized we had to be the ones
to tone this down.
We remembered
that Daddy taught us
to pay attention to
the beautiful things in life.
The heart is a muscle
and joy makes it stronger.

A Woman Disguised as a Normal Person

I watch Mother's hands, so gentle
as she crimps the edge of a pie crust,
stitches together a quilt block,
caresses the piano keys.

I get off the school bus
and tell her what happened that day,
but that is not enough.
She wants to see into my inner life,
to help direct my thoughts.
So I begin to shut her out,
and what she cannot be part of
she wants to destroy.

Mother turns rage outward.
I turn rage inward.
Both of us are battered by circumstance
and unable to walk away.

cont.

I am waiting for someone to appear
who acts like a real mother,
and she longs for a real daughter,
one she could love with all her heart.

Writing Poems

Writing poems
is a pilgrimage, a return,
like the Canada goose
that turns its flock north,
soaring over cliff and forest
in an icy wind
until a circle of trees
or an arrangement of rocks
tells them all
that they have come to the right place.

Legacy

Am I my mother's keeper?
Must I work through the emotions
she finds too hard to bear?
The rage festering in her mind
is a chain letter she can't help passing on
but my sisters and I are choosing not to send it
to the ten people closest to us.

There are graves in our minds,
invisible ones, ancient and toppling over,
where painful memories are hidden.
Under creaking branches
and ragged, stunted shrubbery,
no noise disturbs their sleep
but a vapor trail remains.

cont.

In quiet moments, my faults loom large.
I berate myself for long-ago mistakes.
It would be simpler to distract myself
but I cannot leave this unfinished.
I must deal with it, deal with it.
I have a horror of letting things go,
pretending they never happened.

I put darkness into my poems
— to keep darkness
from seeping into my life.

Of course there were times in the past
when Mother came to herself,
when she remembered how it felt
to be a child, or when she showed us
a fragile shimmer of her best self
and we rushed to forgive her.
But the cease-fire never lasted.

Her inner world is a foreign country.
They do things differently there.

www.ingramcontent.com/pod-product-compliance
Lightning Source LLC
LaVergne TN
LVHW091316080426
835510LV00007B/520